BOOK
For Girls

Smart Words
for
Smart Girls
by
Smart Women

DR. ANDREW SASSANI M.D.

ISBN: 1546791892
ISBN 13: 9781546791898
Library of Congress Control Number: 2017909365
CreateSpace Independent Publishing Platform
North Charleston, South Carolina

Introduction

This book is being published:

- So that all little girls find words of empowering wisdom and encouragements by strong women who were once little girls themselves.
- For our little girls to place it by their bed stands so they will:
    - Read it every night and every morning.
    - Read it with a parent and alone.
    - Go deep and getting lost in the power of these words.
    - Strategize and plan their own dreams.
    - Know that their dreams can come true.
    - Know that there is nothing holding them back.
    - Know that sky is the limit. Or better yet, there is no limit!
    - Know that if they can dream it, they can make it real.

Today's empowered girls,
are tomorrow's world-changers!

*"Don't let anyone tell you that you can't, or
that you're not good enough. You are."*

-Diane Crump, who within seven years of riding became the first woman jockey to ride in the Kentucky Derby in 1970, seen here being protected by police escort entering the race arena due to gender discriminatory attitudes of the time. Read more about this amazing woman and her life story in **Part 3** of the children's book ***Little Girls Powerful Women: How Girls Break Ceilings*** on Amazon at http://amzn.to/2wOLCE4

"As a kid, I had dyslexia. I had a lot of trouble in school and was put into remedial classes. … I'm a professor at John's Hopkins now. Just because you're dyslexic, doesn't mean you can't do the things you want to do."

-Dr. Carol Greider who's dyslexia caused poor standardized test scores and was initially rejected from many graduate programs, won the Nobel Prize in Physiology/Medicine in 2009 and is a Distinguished Professor at Johns Hopkins University, where she is the Director of Molecular Biology and Genetics. Read more about this amazing woman and her life story in the children's book **Little Girls & Nobel Prizes: America's Girl Power** on Amazon at http://amzn.to/2xFQwmf

"I know the world will be a much better place as young women assert themselves, not just in the business world, but in the global arena."

-Zoe Cruz, an immigrant girl who lost her brother as a teenager, persisted through life to become President of Morgan Stanley. *Forbes* magazine listed her as #10 on their "100 Most Powerful Women of the World" in 2006. Read more about this amazing woman and her life story in the children's book **Little Girls Powerful CEOs: From Role-Play to Real-Life** on Amazon at http://amzn.to/2fsPRh0

Dr. Andrew Sassani M.D.

"Until we get equality in education, we won't have equality in society".

-Sonia Sotomayor, who grew up in the low-income public-housing projects of New York and was diagnosed with diabetes at age 7, became the first Hispanic American female justice on the Supreme Court of the United States. Read more about this amazing woman and her life story in **Part 4** of the children's book ***Little Girls Powerful Women: How Girls Break Ceilings*** on Amazon at http://amzn.to/2yCixsV

It took me quite a long time to develop a voice, and now that I have it, I am not going to be silent".

-Madeleine Albright is a politician and diplomat. She is the first woman to have become the United States Secretary of State. She was awarded the Presidential Medal of Freedom in 2012. Madeline serves as chair of Albright Stonebridge Group and as a professor of International Relations at Georgetown University's School of Foreign Service. She also holds a PhD from Columbia University and numerous other honorary degrees. Read more about this amazing woman and her life story in **Part 4** of the children's book ***Little Girls Powerful Women: How Girls Break Ceilings*** on Amazon at http://amzn.to/2yCixsV

"People who end up as 'first' don't actually set out to be first. They set out to do something they love."

-Condoleezza Rice, who as a young child experienced the loss of a friend in an explosion in Alabama, stayed strong and eventually became the first female US national security adviser and first African American female US secretary of state. Read more about this amazing woman and her life story in **Part 4** of the children's book ***Little Girls Powerful Women: How Girls Break Ceilings*** on Amazon at http://amzn.to/2yCixsV

*"Every atom says to every other one "Combine",
and in doing so, they change chaos into order.
When every woman shall say to every other,
"Combine", ...the dragon shall be slain"*

-Francis Willard, the first woman in America to become a College President in 1871. Read more about this amazing woman and her life story in **Part 1** of the children's book ***Little Girls Powerful Women: How Girls Break Ceilings*** on Amazon at http://amzn.to/2y4DAY4

"I work as hard as man, ...but I am robbed as a woman!"

-Ada Kepley is the first woman in America to receive a Law degree in 1870. She was a big supporter of the Women's Rights movement to help other women have the same and equal rights as men. Read more about this amazing woman and her life story in **Part 1** of the children's book *Little Girls Powerful Women: How Girls Break Ceilings* on Amazon at http://amzn.to/2y4DAY4

"At the end of the day, …don't forget that you're a person, don't forget you're a mother, don't forget you're a wife, don't forget you're a daughter. When your job is done, what you're left with is family, friends, and faith."

-Indra Nooyi, Chief Executive Officer (CEO) of Pepsi Co., one of the largest companies in the world with over 185,000 employees in 200 countries. The U.S. News & World Report magazine named her as one of America's Best Leaders and Fortune magazine ranked her the #1 most powerful woman in business for 2009 and 2010. Read more about this amazing woman and her life story in the children's book **Little Girls Powerful CEOs: From Role-Play to Real-Life** on Amazon at http://amzn.to/2fsPRh0

"We cannot all succeed when half of us are held back. We call upon our sisters around the world to be brave – to embrace the strength within themselves and realize their full potential".

"I raise up my voice-not so I can shout but so that those without a voice can be heard...we cannot succeed when half of us are held back".

-Malala Yousafzai. At age 15, Malala was the victim of an attempt to murder her because she was going to school to be educated. She was badly injured, became unconscious and in critical condition. Following her recovery, Malala became a activist for female education, women's rights, and the youngest-ever Nobel Prize winner. She is known for her human rights advocacy. Her advocacy has grown into an international movement fighting against the suppression of children and for the right of all children to education.

*"If your dreams do not scare you,
they are not big enough!"*

- Ellen Johnson Sirleaf, known as Africa's "Iron Lady", became President of Liberia in 2006 as the first elected female head of state in Africa.

"A gender-equal society would be one where the word 'gender' does not exist."

– Gloria Steinem is a journalist, social and political activist, and a nationally recognized leader for women's rights.

*"The future belongs to those who believe
in the beauty of their dreams. "*

- Eleanor Roosevelt was a social activist and the longest-serving First Lady of the United States as the wife of President Franklin D. Roosevelt's four terms in office. She also served as United States Delegate to the United Nations General Assembly from 1945 to 1952. She was known as the "First Lady of the World" because of her human rights efforts and advocacy.

"It takes a great deal of courage to stand up to your enemies, but even more to stand up to your friends".

-J. K. Rowling is the author of "*Harry Potter*" series. She was working as a secretary for Amnesty International when she came up with the idea for *Harry Potter* while on a commuter train to her job. In the 7-year period leading up to finishing her first book, she lost her mother, divorced from her first husband, gave birth to her first child, and lived in poverty relying on state benefits to survive. In addition, she has also written books for adult readers: *The Casual Vacancy, The Cuckoo's Calling, The Silkworm,* and *Career of Evil.* She has won multiple awards, and her books have sold more than 400 million copies.

"Excellence is the best deterrent to racism or sexism. "

-Oprah Winfrey is a philanthropist, producer, owner of multiple media entities, known for The Oprah Winfrey Show, which is the highest-rated program of its kind in history, and called the "Queen of All Media". She is the recipient of the Presidential Medal of Freedom and honorary doctorate degrees from Duke and Harvard. Despite being born into poverty in rural Mississippi to a teenage single mother and later raised in an inner-city Milwaukee neighborhood, she is reportedly the richest African-American billionaire and one of the most influential and powerful women in the world.

"As a woman in science, I sincerely hope that my receiving the Nobel Prize will send a message to young women everywhere that the doors are open to them and they should follow their dreams."

-Dr. Linda Buck at her microscope. In 2004, she won the Nobel Prize in Physiology/Medicine for her important research and contributions to science. She made many discoveries on how smells are detected by the nose and how they are analyzed by the brain. Her research opened the door to important genetic and molecular studies of the biology of smell. Read more about this amazing woman and her life story in the children's book **Little Girls & Nobel Prizes: America's Girl Power** on Amazon at http://amzn.to/2xFQwmf

*"I hope to inspire everyone—especially young
people, women, and young girls all over the world,
...to not give up their dreams and to pursue them...
It may seem impossible to them at times. But I
believe they can realize their dreams if they keep it
in their hearts, nurture it, and look for opportunities
and make those opportunities happen."*

-Anousheh Ansari, Iranian-born immigrant, engineer, and business executive, became the first female astronaut outside a government space program. Read more about this amazing woman and her life story in **Part 4** of the children's book ***Little Girls Powerful Women: How Girls Break Ceilings*** on Amazon at http://amzn.to/2yCixsV

*"Men, their rights, and nothing more;
women, their rights, and nothing less".*

-Susan B. Anthony was a social reformer, abolitionist, and women's rights activist who was a leading figure of the early women's rights movement. She collected anti-slavery petitions at the age of 17 and became an agent of the American Anti-Slavery Society. In 1872, she was arrested for voting and convicted. Susan and Elizabeth Cady Stanton arranged for Congress to be presented with an amendment giving women the right to vote. It eventually became the Nineteenth Amendment to the U.S. Constitution in 1920.

"The best protection any woman can have... is courage".

-Elizabeth Cady Stanton, was a leading figure of the early women's rights movement, social activist, and abolitionist. She is often credited with initiating the first organized women's rights and women's suffrage movements in the United States. Elizabeth Stanton was president of the National Woman Suffrage Association. Elizabeth and Susan B. Anthony arranged for Congress to be presented with an amendment giving women the right to vote. It eventually became the Nineteenth Amendment to the U.S. Constitution in 1920.

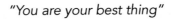

"You are your best thing"

-Toni Morrison, whose parents had escaped the racism of the South, grew up during the Great Depression. Her parents worked multiple jobs to be able to feed Toni and her siblings. When she entered first grade, not only was she the only African American student in the class, but she was the only student who could already read! She became the first African American woman to win a Nobel Prize. Additionally, she is the recipient of Presidential Medal of Freedom, National Humanities Medal, Honorary degrees from fifteen universities, and The Elizabeth Stanton Award by the National Organization for Women (NOW). Read more about this amazing woman and her life story in **Part 3** of the children's book ***Little Girls Powerful Women: How Girls Break Ceilings*** on Amazon at http://amzn.to/2wOLCE4

"Beauty begins the moment you decide to be yourself"

"I don't care what you think about me.
I don't think about you at all".

-Coco Chanel was a fashion designer and businesswoman. She was the founder of the Chanel fashion brand. She is credited with liberating women from the restrictive designs of the 19th century and popularizing a sporty chic as the feminine standard of style in the 20th century. She is the only fashion designer listed on TIME magazine's list of the 100 most influential people of the 20th century.

"The most common way people give up their power is by thinking they don't have any".

-Alice Walker is an author, poet, and social activist. She wrote the great novel *The Color Purple* for which she won the National Book Award and the Pulitzer Prize for Fiction. The book was made into a movie where Oprah Winfrey played the role of Sofia.

"Don't be afraid of hard work. Nothing worthwhile comes easily. Don't let others discourage you or tell you that you can't do it. In my day, I was told women didn't go into chemistry. I saw no reason why we couldn't."

- Gertrude Elinor, child of first-generation immigrant parents who never received a formal PhD, has been recognized as one of the most important scientists and researchers of our time. In 1988, Gertrude Elion shared the Nobel Prize in Physiology or Medicine for discoveries of "important new principles of drug treatment". She is also the first woman to be inducted into the National Inventors Hall of Fame. Read more about this amazing woman and her life story in the children's book **Little Girls & Nobel Prizes: America's Girl Power** on Amazon at http://amzn.to/2xFQwmf

"If you are always trying to be normal, you'll never know how amazing you can be".

"I love to see a young girl go out and grab the world by the lapels. Life's a bitch. You've got to go out and kick ass".

-Maya Angelou was a civil rights activist, poet, memoirist, actress, and social reformer. She published multiple autobiographies, books of essays, poetry, and has been credited with a list of plays, movies, and television shows spanning over 50 years. She was active in the Civil Rights Movement and worked with Martin Luther King Jr. as well as Malcolm X. She received numerous awards and more than 50 honorary degrees. They include a Pulitzer Prize nomination, a Tony Award, three Grammys, awarded the National Medal of Arts, and the Presidential Medal of Freedom.

"Anything is possible. If somebody like me can have the success that I've had, anything is possible. And isn't that a wonderful message to give to your kids!"

-Susan Wojcicki, Chief Executive Officer (CEO) of YouTube. She has been called "the most important person in advertising" and was listed on Time Magazine's 100 most influential people in 2015. She has also been described as "the most powerful woman on the internet". Read more about this amazing woman and her life story in the children's book **Little Girls Powerful CEOs: From Role-Play to Real-Life** on Amazon at http://amzn.to/2fsPRh0

"I never dreamed about success. I worked for it".

-Estée Lauder was an American businesswoman and the co-founder of Estée Lauder cosmetics company. She was the only woman on Time magazine's list of the 20 most influential business geniuses of the 20th century in 1998. Estée Lauder also received the Presidential Medal of Freedom and the Knight class of the Legion of Honor from the Consul General of France, and the first woman to receive the Chevalier Commendation in 1978.

"We must believe in ourselves or no one else will believe in us, ...The world cannot afford the loss of talents of half its people if we are to solve the many problems that beset us."

-Rosalyn Yalow, PhD, American medical scientist who worked two secretarial jobs as a student to pay for college became the winner of Nobel Prize in medicine in 1977 for her role in developing the techniques that made it possible to analyze the blood medical research and treatment purposes. She also received the AMA Scientific Achievement Award, and became the first female recipient of the Albert Lasker Award for Basic Medical Research. She was elected as a Fellow of the American Academy of Arts and Sciences in 1978 and received the National Medal of Science in 1988. Read more about this amazing woman and her life story in the children's book **Little Girls & Nobel Prizes: America's Girl Power** on Amazon at http://amzn.to/2xFQwmf

*"You are more powerful than you know;
you are beautiful just as you are".*

-Melissa Etheridge is a rock-star and social activist. In 2006, at the GLAAD Media Awards, she received the Stephen F. Kolzak Award, which honors openly lesbian, gay, bisexual or transgender media professionals who have made a significant difference in supporting equal rights. Two years before that, Melissa was diagnosed with breast cancer, and underwent surgery and chemotherapy. She has also been honored by having her own star on the Hollywood Walk of Fame.

"America's future will be determined by the home and the school. The child becomes largely what he or she is taught; hence we must watch what we teach and how we live."

- Jane Addams lost her mother at age 2 and four of her siblings by the age of 8. She suffered from tuberculosis of the spine, which caused a crooked back and made her walk with a limp. After undergoing surgery and having to drop out of school, this powerful girl grew up to be the first American woman awarded a Nobel Prize and one of the cofounders of the American Civil Liberties Union (ACLU). Read more about this amazing woman and her life story in **Part 2** of the children's book **Little Girls Powerful Women: How Girls Break Ceilings** on Amazon at http://amzn.to/2wOhokB

"A truly equal world would be one where women ran half our countries and companies, and men ran half our homes".

-Sheryl Sandberg is Chief Operating Officer (COO) of Facebook and founder of LeanIn.org. She is a big supporter of women in leadership roles. Read more about this amazing woman and her life story in the children's book **Little Girls Powerful CEOs: From Role-Play to Real-Life** on Amazon at http://amzn.to/2fsPRh0

"If you know you are on the right track, if you have this inner knowledge, then nobody can turn you off. No matter what they say."

-Barbara McClintock, the first woman from America to win an <u>un</u>shared Nobel Prize in Medicine in 1983. As a child, she had to live with her aunt and uncle because her parents did not have enough money to take care of her. Read more about this amazing woman and her life story in **Part 3** of the children's book **Little Girls Powerful Women: How Girls Break Ceilings** on Amazon at http://amzn.to/2wOLCE4

"I wish you would use all means at your disposal, ...to save and restore the ocean, the blue heart of the planet."

-Sylvia Earle, the first female Chief Scientist of the U.S. National Oceanic and Atmospheric Association. She set the women's record for a world solo dive depth in 1986. Time magazine's First Hero for The Planet, Library of Congress Living Legend, United Nations Champions of the Earth Awardee, Los Angeles Times Woman of the Year in 1970, and Ordained as a Knight of the Most Excellent Order of the Golden Ark by the Prince of the Netherlands. Read more about this amazing woman and her life story in **Part 3** of the children's book ***Little Girls Powerful Women: How Girls Break Ceilings*** on Amazon at http://amzn.to/2wOLCE4

"We can make studies in artificial intelligence. Computer Science can be used to help humans in learning."

-Sister Mary Kenneth Keller, had to fight for her right to use the men-only computer science lab and is the first woman in America to receive a Ph.D. in Computer Science in 1965. Read more about this amazing woman and her life story in **Part 2** of the children's book ***Little Girls Powerful Women: How Girls Break Ceilings*** on Amazon at http://amzn.to/2wOhokB

Dr. Andrew Sassani M.D.

"There is no gender in the law "

-Genevieve Rose Cline, the first woman in America to become a Federal Judge in 1928. A defender of women's equality whenever and wherever she could. Read more about this amazing woman and her life story in **Part 2** of the children's book ***Little Girls Powerful Women: How Girls Break Ceilings*** on Amazon at http://amzn.to/2wOhokB

"The time has passed when a woman should be placed in a position and kept there only while someone else is being groomed for the job."

-Hattie Caraway, the first woman elected to the U.S. Senate in 1932. She won with twice as many votes as the other candidate during the same election which gave us President Franklin D. Roosevelt. Read more about this amazing woman and her life story in **Part 2** of the children's book ***Little Girls Powerful Women: How Girls Break Ceilings*** on Amazon at http://amzn.to/2wOhokB

Dr. Andrew Sassani M.D.

*"Granny gave me strength, dignity, and love. I
learned from an early age that I was somebody."*

-Shirley Chisolm was born to poor immigrant parents who had financial difficulty raising 4 children, partially raised by her grandmother in Barbados, and became the first African American female elected to the US Congress in 1968. Read more about this amazing woman and her life story in **Part 2** of the children's book ***Little Girls Powerful Women: How Girls Break Ceilings*** on Amazon at http://amzn.to/2wOhokB

After being elected the Speaker of the United States House of Representatives:

"This is a historic moment for the women of this country. It is a moment for which we have waited more than 200 years, ...through the many years of struggle to achieve our rights, ... Never losing faith, we worked to redeem the promise of America, that all men and women are created equal. For our daughters and granddaughters, today, we have broken the marble ceiling. For our daughters and our granddaughters, the sky is the limit, anything is possible for them".

-Nancy Pelosi, as the first female Speaker of the U.S. House of Representatives, she became the highest-ranking elected female politician in American history. Forbes magazine has listed her as one of the world's most powerful women. Read more about this amazing woman and her life story in **Part 4** of the children's book **Little Girls Powerful Women: How Girls Break Ceilings** on Amazon at http://amzn.to/2yCixsV

Dr. Andrew Sassani M.D.

After winning the majority popular vote but losing the US presidency based on the Electoral College voting system:

"... I know we have still not shattered that highest and hardest glass ceiling, but some day, someone will, ... and to all the little girls who are watching this, never doubt that you are valuable and powerful and deserving of every chance and opportunity in the world to pursue and achieve your own dreams."

-Hillary Clinton, is the first-ever female winner of majority popular vote in a U.S. presidential election. However, she officially lost the election based on the U.S. Electoral College voting system. She is also a former First Lady, U.S. Senator, and Secretary of State. Following her loss in the general election of November 2016, she started OnwardTogether.org in 2017. The landing page of the website says "Resist, insist, persist, enlist." by Hillary Rodham Clinton. The mission statement includes: "... encouraging people to organize, get involved, and run for office. ...advance progressive values and work to build a brighter future for generations to come."

Afterword

These were some amazingly powerful words, right? I really hope you'll feel empowered and inspired by having read these important words of wisdom. What are your favorite quotes in this book?   What is one of your life-goals you feel passionate about achieving? You can talk about your goals and favorite quotes with a parent or grown-up. I want you to know, that you have the power to accomplish your dreams and life-goals. There are only two things that are required to achieve your dreams: 1) You, and 2) Your determination. Of course, you already have those! Which means:

YOU CAN ACHIEVE YOUR DREAMS!

If you found the words in this book helpful,

- Read them frequently.
- Read them with a parent and alone.
- Strategize and plan your dreams.
- Know that there is nothing holding you back.
- Know that there is no limit to what you can achieve!
- Know that if you can dream it, you can make it real.

To read more about these and other amazingly inspirational women and their life stories, look for these titles on Amazon at http://amzn.to/2hsIE17

- **Little Girls Powerful Women (Parts 1-4):** *How Girls Break Ceilings*
- **Little Girls Powerful CEOs:** *From Role-Play to Real-Life*
- **Little Girls & Nobel Prizes:** *America's Girl Power*

About the Author

Andrew Sassani MD is a married father of two little girls. He is a Harvard trained Board-Certified physician and an Associate Clinical Professor of Psychiatry at a U.S. Medical School. His primary full-time job is being a father and husband. When he is not busy with his family, he is a full-time Medical Director at a national healthcare company. To follow or contact the author via Facebook (@ LittleGirlsPowerfulWomen), click http://bit.ly/2w7ZuVH

Look for other titles on Amazon at http://amzn.to/2hslE17

- **President Sophia: My Road to The White House**
- **Little Girls Powerful Women (Parts 1-4):** *How Girls Break Ceilings*
- **Little Girls Powerful CEOs:** *From Role-Play to Real-Life*
- **Little Girls & Nobel Prizes:** *America's Girl Power*

Made in the USA
Middletown, DE
21 January 2018